MW00931467

Copyright © 2015 Carl Martens

Published by Publish or Perish, Richmond, Virginia

# Preface

**The most interesting Human Being in the Universe has company. It could be you.**

As I read, re-read and refined this section many times (a writer's scourge), it occurred to me that my initial approach to this subject might be too simplistic. But simple is good, right? I'm going with it.

It's been irrefutably proven that reading aloud to children – at any age – even while still in the womb, is absolutely essential and beneficial to their development.

Remember when **you** first started to read aloud in either pre-school or kindergarten? You'd identify a picture, a dog, and written below the picture was the word "DOG". You pronounced the word. This would soon lead to reading several words together out loud – then sentences – then entire paragraphs. WOW, this was a highlight of your introduction to words and reading, and you felt really good about yourself. But, as you progressed into the grades, there was some teacher who ultimately notified you that reading "out loud" was to be discontinued. Ouch! That was so much fun!

***Reading would now be silent!*** Absorb as much as you can – as quickly as you can. But you still feel the need to move your lips when you read. It was amazing how that eagle-eye could see those lips flutter all the way across the room, and that *tyrant teacher* didn't hesitate to tell you it was absolutely not allowed. Darn!

*Maybe I'll become a ventriloquist...*

Guess what? For many of us that may well have been the last time we felt good about reading anything out loud.  Since we were discouraged from doing so, why buck the system?!

> ...for many of us that may well have been the last time we felt good about reading anything out loud.

I'm reminded of a book by Robert Fulghum, *All I Really Need to Know I Learned in Kindergarten.* If reading out loud had been promoted beyond those early years and was then regularly reinforced, this might have been one of the things you learned and retained – like 'flushing the toilet' - and this book may never have been written.

But, for the most part, that didn't happen.

However, some of us were lucky enough to have been introduced to speech club, drama club, debate club or became involved in a music activity like choir or individual voice lessons.

You ask, what does all this have to do with becoming a better speaker?

**EVERYTHING.**

This entire book is based on this one very simple principle.

### *IN ORDER TO BECOME AN EFFECTIVE AND MORE INTERESTING SPEAKER,*

### *ONE MUST FIRST BECOME AN ACCOMPLISHED ORAL READER.*

You must first get a grasp on what interesting reading aloud is all about, and master some of its ignored concepts and secrets many professionals are either unwilling to share, or more accurately, unaware they even exist.  Some may be incorporating a few of these techniques naturally. They're the talented ones – gifted - an incredibly small segment of our professional speaking population.

*Once you've acquired a working relationship of these ideas and techniques, with a positive attitude and practice, they will become an integral part of your improved speaking abilities, either scripted or spontaneous.*

# Contents:

# Chapter 1

## The Basics – Walking & Talking

***The good news.*** This is a relatively short book in terms of pages. You should be able to read it rather quickly.

***The better news.*** If you read it with the intent of studying its content, listening to the brief, supplemental audio recordings and putting into practice what you're learning, the contents of this book will be with you as a constant reminder for a very long time.

This book isn't presumptuous enough to claim to be life-altering. But it does focus on examining a realization that has been within reach since humans began to read, write and speak. Its strength is in its simplicity – and is attainable by virtually all who wish to become more effective communicators, teachers and public speakers. Admit it. We all fall into one of those three categories.

> ...offers practical answers to public speaking and communication short-circuits that we all experience.

***More Than Your Words*** as a statement, represents a paradigm shift. It addresses very little of what's popular and regarded as authoritative in public speaking self-help books published up to this time. But, as you will find, it addresses some fundamental issues, and offers practical answers to public speaking and communication short-circuits that we all experience. These solutions aren't masked in vague references, but solid, straight-forward, concrete applications that you will take away and use the rest of your life, whatever the level of your communication needs. This isn't a bunch of theory and deep analysis stuff about your vocal mechanism, but hands-on stuff you can take to the dance. The best part is that it applies to any level of speaking experience, from high school students to adults who classify themselves as proficient public speakers.

***More Than Your Words?*** If presented as a question, begs an answer. The "More" has to do with your voice, your constant partner associated with who you are, integrated with your mind, spirit, being and a part of something you do regularly. Talk. Some of us entirely too much. You know who you are. Many of us just *love* the sound of our own voice. The problem is, if we could actually hear what we're saying – and how we're saying it – we would probably talk much less. Ever held a microphone (cell phones work well), next to your spouse when he/she is making  strange sounds, you know...snoring...and then play it back the next time they deny making those funny sounds? Well, if you were lucky enough to survive that confrontation, please consider what I'm about to suggest. Keep a phone in your pocket, flip on the audio record function when you're involved in a conversation with someone, on the phone, making a presentation or just checking out at the supermarket. Play it back. That's you kid. That's the way other people hear you. Your first reaction may well be to commit hara-kiri (yes, that's how it's spelled). But, since your beneficiary won't be able to collect insurance benefits if you off yourself, you might consider an alternative.

*It's up to you to change the way you sound.  Become more interesting.  Be less monotonous.  Put some excitement into your conversation.  Get creative.  Sound different.*

It's not going to happen all at once.  It happens gradually.  And here's the neat part.  Nobody will even notice you're doing anything different. *However, the way in which others react to you will be all you need to know that you're making a positive change.* You WILL notice a difference.

> This would be a good time to listen to Track #1 – Introduction. You may access this, as well as the other tracks mentioned in this book by going to **www.ProfitsInPodiumPractices.com**, clicking on the "Book" tab at the top of the home page, and then select Track# 1.  You'll be able to listen to the others in a similar fashion as instructed throughout the remainder of this book.  I was asked if I was going to make a video as well.  No I'm not.  As indicated repeatedly, I will be concentrating on what you hear, not what you see.

There are many books published about public speaking, organizations that support those who have a desire to become better public speakers and workshops on every street corner for executives who want to improve their communication skills, and those of their employee's. This flood of information wouldn't be warranted if the demand weren't there.  Why then is there yet another book entering this already, seemingly saturated market?  Because readers today are not getting some of the basics they need to feel comfortable and be effective.

> **...the proper use of your voice is the fundamental tool in your possession. It's all yours.**

The contents in this book dig deep into the cause and effect of the delivery mechanism. *Your voice.* And how to improve the effectiveness of it. In virtually every publication, this element isn't addressed much or not at all. If it is, it's cloaked in vague references. Sometimes I get the feeling that some authors and instructors think this subject is too personal. Are we unwilling to penetrate this veil of sound, being satisfied using the Band-Aid approach? Well, I'm not satisfied with that, nor should you be. I believe this subject urgently demands attention in this day of tweets, texts, sound bites and instant gratification. The proper use of your voice is the fundamental tool in your possession. It's all yours. It's unique. Nobody else has one like yours. And...you're the only one who can control it!

One of my favorite analogies regarding this approach to speaking vs all the other stuff, is that of a super model who has a beautiful face, spectacular hair, takes tremendous pride in her physical fitness training, spends untold hours on make-up, has a never-ending supply of designer clothes, BUT, has never been taught how to effectively walk down the runway. The whole thing goes south.

Just as the "walk" is so important for a model, your "talk" is equally as important as a speaker. It's your voice. You have to get to know it, understand it, listen to it, and use the tools at your disposal to make the most of it. That's what this book is all about. Digging deep, making changes, sounding different, becoming a more interesting speaker/talker. All the while, making it a fun and meaningful experience.

If you're convinced to continue now that you've almost made it through the first chapter, I suggest that you skip to the end. ADDENDUM – Concerns and Responses (What? The author suggesting you skip to the end? OK - But be certain to come back to this page – good stuff coming up...)

These are questions that have been posed to me over the years – and may well determine how and why you wish to approach reading the contents of this book. I'll provide some short answers – and I'll try to not be annoying and refrain from saying, "Just read the book!"

One more thing. In the Preface, reference is made to "The Most Interesting Human Being in the Universe." This was used partly to get your attention, obviously referring to a very popular beer commercial that's been airing on TV since 2006. (Can't use the Dos Equis actual wording here as it's their trademark.) It was also used because it provides a perfect demonstration of how becoming an "interesting" speaker doesn't have to be about Hollywood directing your every move. You don't have to brag about it or peddle an alcoholic beverage in order to enjoy an exciting persona. Even though it's probably not going to turn you into a Hollywood star, the authentic, but little-known and rarely articulated speaking techniques you'll glean from this book can't help but have a positive effect on your communication efforts, relationships and speaking abilities.

There is a monumental paradigm shift occurring in the public speaking arena.

Learn about it. Adopt it. You don't need Hollywood!

You'll find that there are MANY interesting people out there. You might want to lay claim to being one of them.

# Chapter 2

## The Introvert, Twain & Beer

It started in kindergarten. I was raised in a bilingual home and found myself being escorted to other kindergarten classes to translate for German immigrant children following WWII. It all seemed so natural – two languages – switching easily from one to the other. However, when I was about 8, I began stuttering, partly due to learning two languages simultaneously, partly because of experiencing some trauma with the passing of my father when I was seven. I became self-conscious and turned into somewhat of an introvert – so I concentrated on piano lessons. My fingers were really well coordinated and had no problem with that stuttering thing.

However, there was something about talking/verbalizing that I missed – so I began singing along with the tunes I was playing on the piano. To my surprise, I didn't stutter when I spoke with the addition of a tune. I could sing any words that I had a difficult time speaking. My "B's" were the worst – and the word, "Butter" drove me nuts! But when I put a melody with it, there was absolutely no hesitation.

Relatively soon, I discovered that when I sang a word or phrase first in my head, silently, I could say it without a hint of stuttering. Bottom line, I was able, without outside help (no speech therapist), to virtually eliminate any evidence of my early childhood affliction. It's interesting though, even today, decades later, there are times when I sense some hesitation in my delivery, and it's still affiliated with those bitchy "B" words. I have to take a split second and review what I taught myself so many years ago. It still works. The only reason I mention this, is that it's a first glimpse at the interesting correlation between singing and speaking. More insights and analogies will occur in later chapters.

> ...it's a first glimpse at the interesting correlation between singing and speaking.

Yes, today I consider myself a fairly good oral reader and public speaker. I enjoy it and look forward to the many opportunities to do so. But it isn't nearly as rewarding, nor does it bring me as much joy, as conveying to others what I've learned over the past several decades about how to address some basic speech issues that have stimulated my own personal growth. Interestingly enough, the most enjoyable experiences I had when training sales and marketing teams throughout the years, was observing their successes. I hope that will continue throughout this teaching as well.

### I want to clear up something before continuing.

It seems to be common knowledge (or is it a myth?), that most people are apparently more afraid of public speaking than they are of heights. I hear that all too often.

In case you're one of the supposed majority that share that belief, because you experienced a bit of anxiety or stage fright at one time, or were privileged to have a friend tell you that public speaking was a really, really scary thing, do yourself a favor and read this book with a vengeance. It just might give you an entirely new perspective.

Mark Twain said, "There are two kinds of speakers: those who are nervous and those who are liars." While on the surface it's really quite humorous, it is not a thought that I want to give a sliver of energy to, since it just sets up an entirely negative atmosphere surrounding public speaking. Please understand that I highly revere the oratory prowess of Mr. Twain – his wit and his writing. Intended to be funny, this is one statement that I'd prefer to regard as **only** humorous with no other intended meaning.

Public speaking should be fun, exciting, rewarding – if you only let it. Acquire a few tools, learn a few tricks as outlined in this book, and you'll be able to simplify your entire approach to this activity. Speaking is a discipline. If certain techniques are mastered and a "disciplined" approach is taken when offering a verbal presentation of any kind, while a few jitters are necessary to remain alert and sharp, anything more than that will be absent, and you certainly won't be a 'liar' when asked if you were nervous.

> ...your communication abilities will be enhanced no matter who you're talking to or what the subject matter.

A positive side effect of reading this book and implementing its ideas (how about that, a good side effect for a change), is that your communication abilities will be enhanced no matter who you're talking to or what the subject matter. You'll be amazed at how everyone with whom you come in contact will view you as a new and vibrant communicator, even your spouse, kids and friends. The interesting thing is, they won't have a clue as to why. It will be your little secret. Even your teenagers won't know what's up.

But please remember, all this is based on the simple strategy of learning how to read aloud first. Since many of us are occasionally asked to read in front of an audience – with little or no preparation, I believe there is actually more "fear" in that activity than there is when presenting a prepared speech.

## The Most Interesting Human Being in the Universe

You've undoubtedly seen the commercial for Dos Equis beer, using a similar trademarked phrase as that above, featuring a rugged, handsome man, probably in his seventies. If you haven't, pull it up on You Tube. What makes this beer spokesman so interesting? The ad agency reflects, "He is rich in his stories and experiences, much the way the audience hopes to be in the future." (e.g. "We all want to be like him...")

He's masterfully conjured up by brilliant marketing and advertising people. And, perhaps this stereotype actually does serve a purpose, besides isolating an image that both men and women can relate to positively.

While this is a highly dramatized, sensationalized, sexy, intricately directed presentation – and our eyes and ears are immersed in the spectacle, if the set and costumes were eliminated, all that would be left is a voice. Even that voice alone, with superb direction, manages to convey a striking impression. But is his delivery any more impactful than ours could be by incorporating a few techniques learned in this book? I think not.

Obviously, this gent's appearance, surroundings, feats of strength (when he was younger), and the beautiful women with whom he's frequently seen, certainly don't hurt his image. And, he has at least the hint of an accent. That's always a magnet. The series of commercials, starting in 2006 and continuing to this day, have become an internet meme – and virtually everybody knows the various phrases he utters. The outrageous one-liners offered by the narrator, suggesting super-human abilities, comprise some of the funniest commercials of all time.

So why am I spending time focusing on this gentleman? Because, when you strip all the one-liners away, take away his looks and surroundings, and fire his talented writers, all that remains is a well-schooled actor, superbly cast and directed, but probably no more interesting than anyone else in this universe. He, actor Jonathon Goldsmith, obviously does have a vast theatrical background, and during that training he's certainly learned how to communicate without all the trappings we associate with this particular character...and something tells me that he may be just as interesting without all the effects. But then again, without a director breathing down his throat, giving him every line, move, look and filming take after take – I don't know how he would hold up just reading a prepared speech.

Daily we hear individuals speak without all the advertising gimmicks surrounding their presentation. I remember some who talked for hours on end, and I was totally transfixed by not only what they said, but most importantly, how they said it. Some really didn't have very good posture, or weren't dressed appropriately, or weren't very attractive, or weren't particularly well organized. So how did they keep my attention? By inherently, naturally, utilizing many of the ideas presented in this book. Most of these people don't even know they're doing it. These are the talented few.

My contention here is there are some very "interesting" people in our midst. But, there could be many more if they only learned a few basic concepts prior to incorporating all the "cosmetic" approaches. What's happening in the majority of speech-training applications is analogous to a well-dressed, beautiful model who never learned how to walk. We need to learn how to "walk" first. Bottom line. Then add all the accoutrements. And in our case, that means approaching speech from a different angle – incorporating some basic principles, disciplines, a few tricks and perhaps, occasionally, thinking outside the box.

> My contention here is there are some very "interesting" people in our midst.

Ready to give that beer commercial guy a run for his money?

# Chapter 3

## **Please Pause**

We'll start with a relatively simple concept.

*Silence is golden.*

This is a bit of wisdom originally attributed to ancient Egyptian writings. In 1831, Scottish philosopher and writer, Thomas Carlyle translated the phrase from German into English. No matter where it originated, or who translated it, at some level, we've all, upon occasion, experienced the concept.

The interesting thing is, this applies to so much more than just having a moment or two of silence when you find yourself in a room full of screaming children. Actually, in that example silence might be worth a whole lot more than gold... perhaps like diamonds perched on a mountain of platinum!

In music composition, this "silence" or "pause" is referred to as a "rest," the length of which is determined by the number of beats or portion of beats the silence is to be observed. There's a profound statement that music wouldn't exist without the rest...the space between the notes...the pause.

If that's true in music, could it be true in speech as well?

Even more so.

Speaking without an occasional pause is one of the primary causes of audience boredom, and is always the first "technique" that an individual will mention to me when trying to self-analyze his/her own attempts at improving their oral delivery. A speech or conversation without an occasional pause becomes monotonous, uninteresting, too long or a host of other negatives that could be used to describe meaningless communication.

The simple question is, "where do I take a pause?"

Ah…now there's the rub…where indeed!

Even though we all know the obvious places. Between significant topic changes – possibly paragraphs – chapters – major bullet points in an outline, etc., our tendency is to keep up the speaking momentum that we've established, forgetting that a pause might have a positive effect.

I'm not going to say much more about the obvious pause. You know where they're meant to be. However, I am going to interject a thought that isn't quite so obvious.

The first thing our early training teaches us is that we are required to examine the existing punctuation. Punctuation is definitely important or it would be difficult to understand the written word. Oh…did I say the "written word?" Yup – and here is where you discover one of the most important elements in defining the difference between the written word and the spoken word. Ready?

We were all necessarily brought up learning proper punctuation – when to use a comma, where the period should be – when to use a colon...a semi colon – when to start a new paragraph...and the list goes on and on. This is all important stuff, and its function should not be diminished in the least.

## However...

**All that you ever learned about punctuation in school, must be re-assessed when you're preparing a speech – or reading from a script.**

As I just mentioned, most individuals who are reading out loud at least have an intention to automatically stop...take a breath...employ a pause...at the end of a sentence, at the start of a new paragraph or possibly at the end of a comma. Now, there are certainly times when that may be appropriate, when you remember. **But please expand your thinking!** Your presentation could be much more interesting if you took pauses in places where the audience was least expecting them. The element of surprise. Plus, you could be adding significant meaning to the content. This should be used with subtlety, never over-used, and implemented only when well-rehearsed.

> Your presentation could be much more interesting if you took pauses in places that the audience was least expecting them.

**NOTE:**  Before getting into the meat of this subject, this is as good a place as any to convey one of the most important organizational disciplines you must become accustomed to in order to move forward with the ideas presented in this book.  **Prepare the document you're reading.  This means printing it out in large enough type with double spacing so you can read it easily under existing lighting.  Do not read it from your iPad or Kindle or laptop or any other electronic device.  Why?  Because you're going to mark up the document so that all the techniques you'll be learning here, will be easily followed – and you won't have to rely completely on your memory...at least not yet.**

THERE **WILL** COME A TIME when you can eliminate this activity – and just read or say the words in such a way that all the ideas presented here will come naturally – with minimal rehearsal.  But not yet.  Now you need a printed page, a sharp pencil, an eraser and the ability to apply new thinking to what you've been accustomed to doing your entire life.  **You can do this!**  It might seem like a huge challenge, but making written references on the script will greatly enhance your ability to accept these changes, enable you to practice them and believe down deep that these newly acquired skills will improve your communication skills. It's amazing how natural it will begin to feel.

Once you begin incorporating these techniques and displaying some discipline, the mechanics being implemented in this book will become automatic, and it will always sound like you're "telling the story," rather than "reading it."

One of my over-used but necessary statements when conducting workshops is simply, "Read that story like you weren't **reading** it, but like you were **telling** it – without a script!"

This new way of talking will have more meaning, more excitement, more of *you* actually communicating a valid thought with someone (or a group of people), than you've ever had in the past. The simple benefit is that you'll be understood. People will react to you in a way that you've always hoped they would, but probably infrequently did. They'll actually remember what you said. How incredibly exciting!

...talking will have more meaning, more excitement, more of *you* actually communicating a valid thought...

**Just remember to follow your markings on the script.**

OK – break's over...back to where to take a pause.

Remember, this technique is to be used with finesse. Limit the instances within a paragraph – or even a couple paragraphs where you unleash this powerful attention getter.

If normal punctuation were to be followed in the statement below, the "proper" place to take a pause is after a comma.

*"It wasn't so much a matter of discovering, but connecting the dots."*

Your inclination would be to take a short pause, or "catch" after the word "discovering." You would then follow by saying the words that follow "but connecting the dots."

Consider this. Don't take a break after "discovering", instead, flow easily and directly into the word "but," **THEN TAKE A PAUSE**.

"It wasn't so much a matter of discovering, **but** connecting the dots."

When reading this out loud, you'll want to give "but", a bit of a lift, an upturn in your inflection on the word "but." Then take a short pause, and continue. Try it.

When some of us had the opportunity to read to our young children or grandchildren, it was relatively easy to put a lilt in our voice – to relate to the child in a way that they would be more receptive. Try to remember those days, but now you'll be using more intelligent techniques, as introduced in this book, since you'll probably be speaking to adults.

What does this do? It creates a sort of dramatic build-up to what comes after the word "but." The audience is subconsciously thinking "but what...what's coming next? I want to know. Is it something exciting?" This is a word, belonging to a whole group of words, generally referred to as "transition or connecting words," that I designate as **ACTION WORDS**. They're so underrated! They're really a lot more important than you ever thought! When you're reading silently, you certainly wouldn't phrase the words like I'm suggesting. Silent reading needs a certain order and discipline all its own in order for the reader to assimilate easily and quickly what is written. ***But now you're reading for the benefit of other's understanding, not yours.*** (**You** had better already understand it!)

Words like **but, and, because, while, then, when** and a bunch more that we tend to throw away (in our current understanding, they're unimportant...but apparently necessary to convey a meaning), climb to the head of the class when it comes to oral interpretation of the written word. They're the runt of the litter, that now becomes the loveable and powerful pet we always knew they could be.

Let's look at another example:

"The waves were getting higher and higher, when the boat lost all control."

Normally the pause (while reading silently) would come naturally after the word "higher."

But read it out loud – and there is so much more impact if the pause is taken after "when."

"The waves were getting higher and higher **when**, the boat lost all control."

Find a passage in a book, newspaper, magazine – and read it silently first. Then find a comma or two – see if the word following that comma is what I refer to as an action word. Cross out the comma, and place it after the word instead. Now read it out loud. Practice it a few times so that it begins to sound natural. It will probably require that you alter the inflection a bit. If you can hear yourself, it will sound different...strange. Pick up that cell phone and record yourself reading it both ways. Do you hear the difference? Is it something you can live with? (Not your voice, silly,...you've got to live with that...get over it.) I'm talking about the difference in the way the passage sounds. Does it convey a more vivid meaning? Is it more interesting? If not, don't use it in this instance. Or, practice until it sounds the way you intended.

Remember what I said. This can be over-used, and all of a sudden you're viewed as some kind of a speaking weirdo. So, everything in moderation, right?

...while practicing, screw moderation!

A word of advice. Practice this several times a day. Find different documents, different genres, subjects that interest you – and conduct this same exercise. For this exercise, even though I have said that everything should be done in moderation, while practicing, screw moderation! Don't be afraid to over-do this inflection thing when you're alone in your practice chambers. You've got to make some changes, and practicing with exaggeration, in the privacy of your own space, will allow you to do so with greater speed.

If you haven't guessed, this is part of that discipline stuff.

---

**NOTE:**  Although it's extremely important to learn the reasons behind making these changes, sometimes hearing the implementation of the process can help a great deal.  As such, here is a recording of these two examples.  Please access Track # 2 – Pause on the website.  Again, that's **www.ProfitsInPodiumPractices.com**, click on "Book" at top and go to Track #2.

---

NOTES:

# Chapter 4

## The Rhythm Method...This One Works!

You mean there's one that doesn't?  Hmmmmm...

Again, we'll take a look at another rather simple application when it comes to effective reading/speaking.

Let's focus on one of the most common speaking faux pas that shouts "BORING!"

We've all experienced speakers that found their own "speed control," resulting in so much monotony, our minds easily wandered to more stimulating playgrounds.  Our eyes flapped shut and our chin landed on our chest.  Result?  Nothing absorbed.  Stiff neck.

When the rhythm remains the same for too long a period, without breaking it up with a pause, or changing the rhythm, the audience tends to tune out.  It doesn't have to be an audience of more than one. Have you ever seen your spouse's eyes glaze over when you were speaking – and you asked rather emphatically, "Are you listening to me?"  That conversation may not have ended well.

Compare speaking with dancing.  If you're doing a fox trot where the rhythm is typically 2 or 4 counts to a measure, you count, 1,2,3,4, measure after measure, for the entire length of the dance.  This sounds rather boring in and of itself, but remember, you have movement, costumes and music to make the presentation more interesting.  So, when dancing, you can get by with one constant rhythm.  Actually, some of the more modern choreography incorporates different rhythms within the same dance – really mixes things up a bit, and adds even more interest.

Fortunately, I'm not advocating that you dance around the stage while giving a speech or tap dance your way about the kitchen when communicating with your spouse. Doing this, along with using the legitimate ideas you'll be implementing because of reading this book, would definitely place you in the "weird" category. Don't do that.

How then, can you vary the rhythm while speaking?

**You just happen to be both the soloist and conductor. You're in charge.**

It's not as much about changing the rhythm as it is changing the pace in which you're delivering the message. Slight changes that incorporate speaking more slowly during some passages, while speeding things up a bit in others, keeps things interesting and the audience on their toes. In music, there's a word, **"Rubato."** This is defined as: "a musical term referring to expressive and rhythmic freedom by a slight speeding up and then slowing down of the tempo of a piece of music at the discretion of the soloist or the conductor." This action, more than anything else regarding pace, has a direct impact on your oral reading and speaking presentation, and you'll be taking the first step in eliminating boredom. You just happen to be both the soloist and conductor. You're in charge.

Consider this passage from Maya Angelou's "Courage."

"...**you need courage, and that doesn't mean the battlefield, or picking up a 100lb weight and running into battle – I don't mean that, I mean the courage inside yourself, it allows you to see yourself in other human beings.**"

You might want to start out on a moderate pace – then speeding it up a bit starting with "...or picking up a 100lb weight," and then slowing way down beginning with "...I don't mean that, I mean..." Go ahead, mark up this passage so you'll understand your hieroglyphics. Then practice.

Access Track # 3 – Rubato –
www.ProfitsInPodiumPractices.com

One specific area a change in tempo is particularly effective, is when the author has elected to list a series of words with commas separating them. Rather than thinking logically here, taking a break between each word, you might consider taking a slight break after the first word, and then read then next few more quickly – possibly slowing down a bit on the last couple. Again, the audience will be kept on their toes – and will actually absorb the series of words better than if each word were laboriously pronounced within a constant rhythmic pattern.

Again, it gives you a chance to play. Playing is fun, especially when it benefits everyone.

Look at this sentence. "She had a glorious time viewing the tulips, roses, lilacs, geraniums, pansies, begonias and even the dandelions." In this case, rather than taking the same length break between each word, you might want to take a slight pause after "tulips" – and possibly another after "roses." But then, run the rest quickly together – ending with a pause after *(get that?...after, not before!)*, the "and". Try it. Read it out loud several times. Play with it. Record different versions. Play them back. What works? What doesn't?

I've recorded a couple of versions of this sentence.

Access <u>Track # 4 – Rhythm</u> –
www.ProfitsInPodiumPractices.com

This strategy doesn't work every time, but when a series of words is listed, especially for effect and not necessarily for any serious content, it certainly makes things more interesting, both for the reader and the audience. Again, it gives you a chance to play. Playing is so necessary, especially when it benefits everyone.

# Chapter 5

## **Smile**

Don't be misled. This isn't as easy as it sounds. Some individuals are just not prone to smiling much – or at all in some cases.

Now, please don't conjure up a picture of the Miss America Pageant – with everyone having a plastic, all white teeth, painted-on-smile during the entire show.

Smiles are to be used sparingly when speaking. Use them to change a feeling within the document or context of the speech – to support a bit of wit – or perhaps reacting conservatively to something actually funny, but without bursting into an irritating guffaw.

Remember, there are times when slight changes are all that's necessary...even life-altering. Consider when driving your car down a highway at 70 MPH. You're negotiating a slight curve to the left. There's a bridge abutment crossing the highway in about 1000 feet. Do you suddenly jolt the wheel to the left to account for the curve, or do you turn the wheel very, very slightly to avoid a disaster? The same principal applies to your smile.

A little is all you need.

When I was conducting training classes for telephone etiquette many years ago, I had a room full of perspective employees, each of them thinking they had pretty good telephone skills. I asked them to read a simple script – the way they might read it in answering a phone call. Each person's reading was recorded. Then I asked them to read the same script, only this time with a smile on their face.

"But I can't think of anything funny," was a frequent reply.

Doesn't matter. Just paint on a smile – you know, Miss America Pageant - with the corners of your mouth turned up – teeth showing – eyes sparkling. I know, it's all fake – but just try it. (This is the only time I have ever advocated this method...I promise.)

> Blank stares, glances through the windows to the outside and restlessness were all pretty good indicators that I race losing them.

A second round of recordings were made, this time with that pasted-on smile.

Without exception, each person was astounded at how different they sounded between the two recordings. The smile inspired a welcoming tone in their voice – without exception.

A smile just does something. What? I don't have a scientific explanation for it – and if I did, it probably wouldn't be very interesting. Just know, that there is a different energy exuded – even over the phone. When "in person," the effect is even greater. That's when you want to make certain your smile is genuine. I can personally remember a couple times when I felt I was losing an audience. Blank stares, glances through the windows and restlessness were all pretty good indicators that I was losing them and needed to do something. Fast. All I did was find a passage where I could get by with exhibiting a smile. It was amazing how virtually everybody snapped to attention, looked up and once again connected.

This reminds me of one person who had a universally positive effect on the world population in the early and mid-1900s. Charlie Chaplin. He was born in 1889, had a dynamic film career spanning 75 years, during which he made people smile on a regular basis. Something many people don't know about Mr. Chaplin, is that he actually wrote the music (words added in 1954) to the song *"Smile."*

The first two lines of the song begin, *"Smile, though your heart is aching. Smile even when it's breaking."*

If you're having a problem thinking of a reason to smile, remember Charlie's advice. It's worked for me many times. Even when I wasn't faced with talking or giving a speech, just the act of smiling had a positive effect on my attitude – and I began to feel better...virtually immediately. Here's the point. If you're feeling good, it's much more likely that the person or people you're talking to will feel good as well, even if there's a little "make believe" involved. Amazing how that works!

Your next task will be to find an article in which you can isolate a passage, phrase, sentence where you might want to incorporate a smile in your presentation. Here's a brief example of an opening statement to a lecture. Consider smiling between the parentheses. If this is too much for you, try it in just one of the sections. In these cases, the content isn't really "funny" – but can be considered a bit amusing – and will stand out if a smile envelopes the words.

("Thank you for showing up today.) You all have busy schedules, and many choices as to how you spend your time. (My goal for you, very simply, is to make the next hour unforgettable.)

It's difficult for many to believe they don't have adequate speaking skills, let along reading skills. But is it a wonder? (Verbal skills have been kicked in the teeth during the past couple decades – with the instant gratification of texting – and tweeting) – culminating in a century-old decay of day-to-day oral communication."

There's a subtlety involved that, as I mentioned at the beginning of this chapter, isn't necessarily all that easy – but it IS EFFECTIVE!

> Access different interpretations - Track # 5 –Smile –
> www.ProfitsInPodiumPractices.com

This is a good place to mention a habit that affects many of us. We talk too fast. Day in and day out – talking on the phone, talking to our kids, talking to our employees or peers, *and...when making speeches!* Slow down. Again, easier said than done. This will take repeated practice – like training for a marathon – every day – recording what you're doing – comparing it with what you recorded a week ago – a month ago.

NOTE: When incorporating a smile in your presentation, a **slower pace** will help accentuate this subtle change – and the response will be much more effective and rewarding.

NOTES:

# Chapter 6

## Volume is the Spice of Life

Wait a minute. I thought the cliché used the word "Variety" not "Volume."

Traditionally it is. But for the sake of making this book a little more controversial, let's pretend that it's actually volume. Play along with me on this. OK?

You've set your clock radio for 6 AM. You've chosen the radio station, iPad or CD music to bring you back to consciousness. Have you set the volume on "high?" Don't think so – unless you screwed up - in which case you've awakened with a jolt. At least you know you have a heart.

In this case the volume is set rather low. It's much more appropriate for the occasion.

You're now heading home, long commute, after a full day at work. The traffic is crawling and you really want to be home – reclining – sipping a glass of wine – playing with the kids – whatever. But you have 20 miles yet to go, and it will probably take another hour at the pace you're going. The radio is switched on. Is it soft, soothing music you'll be listening to? Well, maybe at first, just to let you know there's something less hectic than what you've experienced during the past 8 hours. However, soon the eye lids tend to sag, and you need more that that cup of coffee left over from the morning commute. TURN UP THE

VOLUME! Go ahead, kill some of those little hair things in your ears, it's better than dosing off at the wheel. Right?

The point of all this is to emphasize there's always a place for a variety of volumes in your life. This is something of which most of us are conscious naturally, instinctively. However, when giving a talk, a speech, a training class or having a one-on-one conversation with a friend, the issue of vocal volume is seldom considered.

This singular aspect of effective speech, however, can have more impact than anything else. It takes your speaking from "boring" to "interesting" virtually instantaneously.

And, you can do it whether you're in a room of a thousand (with the use of a good microphone), in a gathering of a half a dozen or in a friendly conversation with your friend.

**Side bar:** Isn't it interesting that politicians have never caught on to this. They tend to be either loud, louder or continuously soft. Just think of the impact they would have if they incorporated some dynamics in their presentation. PA systems today will handle just about anything. I don't understand.

Moving on.

There are a couple of hard and fast rules when it comes to volume.

1.  The "normal" volume level of a speaker should always be such that it's possible to get louder, and at the same time possible to get softer.

2. It's usually more impactful to deviate from the normal volume level to present a thought with a quiet intensity than it is to be bombastically loud. First, loud tends to hurt our sensitive ears while insulting our intelligence. Soft enlists our curiosity, we sit on the edge of our seat and we're more involved.

However, the most important rule about volume happens to concentrate on the word "Soft." There are two softs in our lives. There is the intimate soft, experienced between two romantically involved people, or the whispering in a library. And then there is the other soft, the one in which we have a great interest. This is the INTENSE SOFT. This is the stage whisper (a whisper from a stage that, with enough intensity, breath support, energy and projection, reaches the last row in the balcony). This is the utterance of something so important that an audience will be immediately brought back from any wayward mind games.

The changing of volume when speaking must be accomplished with a certain amount of finesse. Very rarely will you be able to, or want to, change from a low volume to a high volume instantaneously. Unless, of course you really want to irritate your audience – perhaps bringing them to the brink of having a heart attack. A slow increase in volume over several words or phrases can be very effective.

Another successful use of volume alteration is the use of **soft intensity**.

I'll demonstrate these volume changes by reading the "Side Bar" noted above.

Access <u>Track # 6 – Volume</u> –
www.ProfitsInPodiumPractices.com

# Chapter 7

## "That Was a Bit Pitchy"

We've all listened to TV and Film personalities who were judging a singing competition make that comment at least once. What they're referring to is that the singer didn't quite reach an intended note or two during their song – they were flat – or possibly over-shot that intended note – a little sharp. Either way, they didn't hit the note squarely – right on the button. For some of us, our ears aren't sensitive enough to enable us to know what actually occurred. We just have a sense that something didn't sound quite right.

> Pay absolutely no attention to what they're saying – but rather in how they're saying it.

The good news is you really don't have to have perfect pitch, or even such a keen sense of pitch to hear when somebody is singing off key a bit. And the better news is you don't even have to learn how to sing or read music to derive great benefits from reading this section! However, you DO have to be able to distinguish when someone is repeatedly ending a phrase, a sentence or a paragraph on the same pitch...or close to the same pitch.

What does this sound like? MONOTONOUS! BORING!

The only area where this might be acceptable, and actually desirable – since the advertisers really don't want to emphasize the negatives and nobody listens anyway – are the TV ads for various medications where the dreadful side effects take up two thirds of the commercial time. (There's just gotta be a law against all those!)

This chapter is really all about you going on field trips. In fact, you'll want to go on these field trips as often as you possibly can. The best part? You don't have to leave the comfort of your home or car to do this. Just listen to the radio or sit in front of the boob tube and listen to news commentators, preferably local – either network TV, Cable or PBS.

Listen to these people differently than you've ever listened to them before. Pay absolutely no attention to what they're saying – but rather to how they're saying it. If you want to listen for content, record the program, then play it back twice (or more), and listen for content the first time, then listen to their delivery.

Listen carefully to the very end of each phrase, sentence, or paragraph. I mean the very, very end...the last sound that comes from their lips prior to continuing onto another phrase, sentence, paragraph or thought. Listen to the sound of their voice before they pause for a comma or period.

Rather shortly, you'll discover that the vast majority of commentators tend to end these phrases on the same, or almost the same pitch. It happens most frequently when the speaker is reading from a script or teleprompter. (And that's most of the time.) You'll probably listen to quite a few before you're really able to identify those boring endings. Give it time, you will. Then, intermixed with the majority will be the occasional sound that grabs you – someone actually had some variety in the way they ended phrases. It will sound refreshing – adding interest to whatever they were talking about.

For your entertainment pleasure…ahem…I've recorded a passage in two different ways. The first is where I end each phrase on the same pitch – and the second is where I consciously make a decision to vary the pitch.

> Access Track # 7 – Pitch –
> www.ProfitsInPodiumPractices.com

Can you hear the difference?

Another place to practice this "discernment" (remember, we're never judgmental…), is at church, or a public meeting, seminar, or any type of presentation. Soon you'll be able to retain the content of message while at the same time evaluating the delivery. Closest thing to multi-tasking I've ever been able to accomplish.

If you do this right, your awareness will be altered…for life. You might even go as far as to pretend you were giving the speech/talk/reading – and silently determine how **you** might have done something different to make it sound more interesting.

**Word of caution.** While becoming more aware of this unfortunate verbal pattern in others, that same awareness can cause you to fixate on being judgmental. Please just observe, discern and store it for future access – comparing it to your own delivery.

This one little adjustment will actually give you a huge step up in as you climb that mountain in becoming one of the "Most Interesting Human Beings in the Universe!"

NOTES:

# Chapter 8

## A Phrase and a Roller Coaster

I love roller coasters. But what does a roller coaster have to do with a phrase? And what *is* a "Phrase" anyway?

As we enjoy that roller coaster slow climb to the top, here's something to chew on.

This is actually my favorite chapter because, if you, the reader/student learns and puts into practice the material presented here, you will have incorporated teachings in virtually all the other chapters. However, it can also be the most difficult to assimilate, particularly if you have a hard time hearing how you sound, ***as you talk***. Got that? You must be able to listen to yourself as you talk! Since that subject will be addressed in the next chapter, I won't say anything more at this time. Just know that **LISTENING TO YOURSELF** is one of the most important aspects of becoming a good speaker. I want you to take a look at the paragraph below. This hopefully contains some subject matter that you can get into, and read with some emotion. There are several opportunities to emphasize specific words, and you'll probably want to pounce on them, believing that in so doing you are communicating to the best of your ability.

Go on, read it silently first, then jump right in and read it out loud...AND RECORD WHAT YOU'RE READING ON YOUR CELL PHONE!

I've suggested recording yourself previously, and I know what you might be thinking. *"I'm not going to do that...trying to figure out how to record on my cell phone...ugh...besides...that takes time...time I don't have right now...so I'll just read it silently. I understand what this is all about!"*

OK, don't read it out loud. But you must make a choice. One is to put this book down and schedule another time to record when you're in a more receptive frame of mind or you won't feel as rushed. (And before you come back, you might want to figure out how to use your cell phone.) Another choice is to throw this book in the garbage. You're done. This happens to be one of the most important chapters in the whole book. **You've come this far.** It would be sad if you quit now. And then, another choice might be to really dig into this chapter with all your might – and become so comfortable with its contents, that you could actually teach somebody else what you've learned. This choice, along with

A one-time lecture on this subject, while possibly being entertaining, is virtually useless and will be of long-term benefit to no one.

possibly attending a workshop presented by an organization or place of employment (at which you will obviously be a STAR student), might be the best – although probably not the most immediately satisfying. Our workshops, once a week for 2 hours, take place over a period of usually 5 weeks, during which a layering takes place, avoiding being bombarded with so much information at once that you're overwhelmed. We also have participant interaction where demonstrations reinforce the tenets of good speech-making. You will always have a chance to practice. A one-time lecture on this subject, while possibly being entertaining, is virtually useless and will be of long-term benefit to no one.

At the beginning, I mentioned that this book is relatively short. However, if you really want to assimilate as much information as possible, enabling you to implement the various techniques, it could easily take you several weeks to complete.

Please read and record one of my favorite quotes of Maya Angelou.

**"Courage is the most important of all the virtues because without courage you cannot practice any other virtue consistently. You can be anything erratically; kind, fair, true, generous, loving...but to be that thing time after time, you need courage, and that doesn't mean the battlefield, or picking up a 100lb weight and running into battle – I don't mean that, I mean the courage inside yourself, it allows you to see yourself in other human beings."**

*Maya Angelou*

Hey! That roller coaster just reached the top. Time for that heart popping plunge! Breathe!

*Ahhhh...Believe it or not, that's not why you're taking this ride!* What happens after the plunge? Roller coasters on which I've ridden now begin a series of small climes and similar descents. Up and down, up and down, jolts around corners – left and then right.

Let's translate this to reading.

> **Once you master this area, you will have an entirely new and fresh take on what effective speaking is all about.**

Now, listen to that passage you just recorded. Go ahead, listen. Yes, that's you...we've already had that discussion. Perhaps the following is a proper assessment of what you're hearing?

Your voice goes up and down, up and down, accenting certain words, falling off on others – then highlighting others and dismissing others – all haphazardly, or at best, employing accents on words you thought were important. This is the part of your delivery when reading out loud that you MUST AVOID! A roller coaster doesn't understand the idea of "phrasing." But you do...or soon will. **Really important.**

This is the most influential of all the techniques contained in the book. Once you master this area, you will have an entirely new and fresh take on what effective speaking is all about, and will be able to incorporate this technique in virtually all of your speaking, whether in a group setting, or one-on-one.

I said this will be challenging. ***But you can do it! I know you can!*** I've actually spent lots of time with relatively good speakers...those who have many of the other elements mentioned here down pat...and many of ***them*** have a difficult time understanding and implementing changes that involve "Phrasing." This area really stands alone, and you're on equal footing with all the rest.

I believe the source and subsequent examples of much *ineffective* speech comes from TV news broadcasters. (OK, if you're one of those, I apologize...nothing against you personally, but more likely your training and the station management you work for.) Ever notice how they tend to sensationalize everything? How do they do this? They emphasize words that they believe will elicit a reaction from their audience – sort of a cheap shot at making things sound important – meant to help ratings – gearing their delivery (and much of their content), to a fifth grade level of communication and interest. Do they read like a roller coaster? Many of them, much of the time.

You may already know what I'm going to say next. **DON'T READ ONE WORD AT A TIME.** This allows for the inevitable "punched word" and the resulting vacuum after it. Read in groups of words – or *PHRASES!*

I remember well what my high school sophomore English teacher taught me. "Every word is important. English is a great language if used properly." As such, all words have some use in the sentence or "phrase." Now, every word can't have nearly the same individual value or impact, but they are all useful in conveying the intended meaning of the whole. If you've ever participated in presenting a play, and had to memorize lines, you immediately realized how each word is so important in conveying the intended meaning. The playwright has very specific ideas in mind.

"Every word is important. English is a great language if used properly."

You, as an actor, must be the mouthpiece of the author. (I was always good at auditions, reading the part. It's the memorization part that proved to be the challenge...ugh.) Granted, there is a lot of inferior writing out there – so please, don't apply my remarks to comic books, dime novels or super-market check-out stand tabloids. I'm referring to respected writing of acclaimed novels, major newspaper editorials, educational texts, news and spiritual periodicals and much of what you'll find in your public library.

So, if every word is important, how do you convey the meaning of a sentence or "phrase" in such a way as to not punch supposedly important words? This is where we need to inspect the meaning of the word "phrase."

The Webster definition of phrase as it applies to literature is: *a small group of words standing together as a conceptual unit, typically forming a component of a clause.*

A phrase can be as short as two words, or an entire sentence. It all depends on what you decide are the group of words that constitute the intended, communicated meaning.

Ok, so we have a group a words. Yea. Now what?

Let's briefly enter the world of music where it's much easier to understand the value and effects of a phrase.

Again, you won't have to read music – or learn how to play the violin (thank God). Just pay attention to the next few paragraphs and you'll know as much about phrasing as many professional musicians…well, almost…at least enough to apply it to speaking.

This is a quote that I find most enlightening. *"Phrasing can never be made a mechanical process, without perverting and artificializing the whole manner of delivery."*

— **Samuel Silas Curry; Lessons in vocal expression**

Since we've been focusing on lots of rather mechanical, technical issues up to this point, why are we now talking about phrasing not being mechanical? Because it isn't. Phrasing works hand in hand with putting the **heart** into your **talk**. Phrasing, probably more than any other technique, is where you'll really be able to connect with your audience. They'll understand you better, they'll believe you more and they'll remember what you've said longer when you incorporate good phrasing. The connection which you'll be able to create combining Heart with Authenticity and Phrasing will put you on the "believable and interesting list" faster than anything I know.

**Kristi Hedges** is a columnist for Forbes Magazine. Besides that, through the years, she has been a trainer for many public speaking workshops designed for corporate executives. One of her main emphases today, after spending many hours on the training side, is contained in this one statement.

"We are used to observing a diverse set of human behaviors, and have adapted well to reading authenticity. We readily sniff out a person who cares, and we hone in on that. Authenticity creates a trust bond and establishes credibility. The rest becomes superfluous."

"The rest" that she refers to as being superfluous has to do with "piles of 'correct' postures, gestures, and speech effects to practice. Don't tilt your head! Stand up straight! Don't pace too much! Walk more! Make eye contact with more people! Make eye contact with a few people! Gesture bigger! Gesture smaller!"

"...are generally over-emphasized too early in the training process." Even though these other areas have some bearing on audience retention, they are generally over-emphasized too early in the training process. It's analogous to putting a beginning skier on a Black Diamond slope their first time out. Your instructor says, "later we'll learn the fundamentals of skiing," while you're lying in the hospital with a broken leg, possibly never to glide down that hill again.

Another analogy addresses how one begins to rehearse for a play. The first thing an actor does is read his/her lines. Then he or she attacks the memorization mode while the blocking, when and where to gesture, move, body language are all inserted into the package. Notice, we didn't start with the gestures first. Ya gotta know your lines!

So many speakers have had similar parallel experiences – being given advice that does nothing to really connect him/her with the audience. It just doesn't work for them, and they never attempt to give another presentation. Sad.

Back to phrasing.

Phrasing is something that, whether you're reading, speaking, playing an instrument, or singing, must have a genuine "feel" to it – a stroke of emotion tied to it. In music, it can mean a simple and gradual increase in volume for the first part of the phrase, and then a gradual decrease in volume for the second part of the phrase. A crescendo followed by a decrescendo for you musical types...

Sing with me. *"Happy Birthday to you."* Slowly. That's enough, don't create a scene. (You may want to go where you'll be alone...) Start rather quietly on the word "Happy" – build your volume on "Birthday" – then start to decrease your volume on "to" – until you gently caress the word "you." Remember how Marilyn Monroe sang the word "You?" OK...bad example. In this case the "phrase" would be a curved line, shaped like a rainbow, sitting above the words, starting above the "H" in "Happy" – and ending over the "u" in "You."

Happy Birthday to You.

Phrase marks like this (not multicolored like a rainbow, but just as impressive), are very common in virtually all types of music. Many times they're accompanied by dynamic markings, indicating when to be soft, and when to be louder. But the bottom line is, a phrase is used to convey a subtle meaning – which generally provides an emotional link between the performer (speaker) and the audience. Isn't this better than hitting the word "Birthday," virtually ignoring all the other words? Reminds me of a bull in a China shop.

I was out-voted on this. I really didn't want to record this section – but here it is. The important thing to remember is this is a very, very simplistic example of phrasing.

Access <u>Track # 8 – Happy Birthday</u> –
www.ProfitsInPodiumPractices.com

Unfortunately, we don't have phrase marks to refer to when interpreting the written word. We need to insert them ourselves. And remember, punctuation of the spoken word is different than the written word. This is why it's imperative that you print out what you're reading and use a pencil to indicate what group of words you want to phrase.

When you incorporate a phrase in a sentence, it takes away the necessity for accenting or "pouncing" on a particular word. Integrate the word that you may be inclined to accent into a meaningful phrase. The effect, and the sound to the listener will be much more intense and have a more lasting impact.

It's now your turn again.

Turn on that recorder and read the passage you read earlier.

I've printed it again below (a more complete version), only this time with markings that indicate where phrasing might be appropriate. At this point, over-emphasize the beginning and ending of each phrase. Just make certain that a single word within that phrase isn't punched or accented in an attempt to convey the intended meaning.

Read.

**"[Courage is the most important of all the virtues because] [without courage you cannot practice any other virtue consistently.] [You can be anything erratically;] [kind, fair, true, generous, loving...but] [to be that thing time after time,] [you need courage,] [and that doesn't mean the battlefield, or picking up a 100lb weight and running into battle] – [I don't mean that,] [I mean the courage inside yourself,] [it allows you to see yourself in other human beings."]**

*Maya Angelou*

Did you notice that this entire paragraph is made up of phrases? Yes. That's the way it works. No word within a sentence should stand alone...unless, of course, that sentence consists of only one word...like "Yes." A no-brainer.

Now listen to yourself. Are you still sounding like a roller coaster, or have you smoothed out your delivery somewhat? If so, congratulations! While it's difficult conveying this phrasing thing without actually being able to hear what it sounds like, it is possible, and with a little practice, you can hammer out this chapter as easily as the other chapters.

However, I want you to feel like you've succeeded – and that you understand exactly what I've been demonstrating with the written word.

Access Track # 9 – Angelou –
www.ProfitsInPodiumPractices.com

As you're listening to the second recording with the implementation of phrasing, please try to identify some of the other elements presented in this book as well. Can you hear where a change in dynamics, pause, rhythm, pace and a smile was used? Feel free to use this as a model when preparing a speech or a reading.

Now that you've heard the difference, try recording yourself again, using effective phrasing.

Please keep in mind that a phrase doesn't always have to look like a rainbow. It can have other gentle curves in it – like a gentle wave, with the curve going up at the end of the phrase. The important thing to remember is to always make it smooth – no sudden jerks or punches...usually. Ah yes, there are exceptions to every rule. Even this one. (Addressing the exceptions would be like presenting a doctoral thesis – and neither one of us needs or wants that at this point. Unnecessary.)

NOTES:

# Chapter 9

## Increase Your Listening Quotient

This entire book has been devoted to speaking – talking – producing sounds through the use of your diaphragm, vocal cords and mouth formation. There's an incredible amount of additional information that could be imparted here. However, that's been done before...many times...many books...many websites, many classes/lectures/workshops. While it's important for every speaker to understand the rudiments of sound production, you're not going to get it here. Google "Diaphragm use in speaking," or "Vocal Cords & speech," or "Pronunciation and Mouth Formation." You'll be faced with a mountain of offerings.

This chapter is about listening.

You've heard the adage many times – "God gave us two ears but only one mouth, so listen twice as much as you speak."

Amen.

This concept will now be taken to an entirely new level.

We always want to listen to others intently, without thinking what our next response will be, thereby restricting our listening ability. But what I'm presenting here is different. *We must learn how to listen to ourselves.*

You've undoubtedly heard yourself on recordings, videos or memos you've sent to yourself. Or, perhaps your first experience was listening to yourself reading the Maya Angelou quote in this book. Exciting, no?

Well, this is only the first step in being able to really listen to yourself. What you want to accomplish in this talking/speaking thing is the ability to listen to yourself, *as you're speaking*. WOW! How do you do that?

Practice...Listen...

Practice, practice, practice...Listen, Listen, Listen.

Use that cell phone recorder again. This time, find a short phrase that you can easily memorize. Something like *"This exercise will be the most exciting part of my training this week."*

Record it, speaking with as much meaning as you can muster. Just say it once. Then wait a few seconds, and repeat it, using exactly the same inflections that you used the first time without referring to your script. Listen to both recordings. Are they similar? Record it again. This time ham it up a bit – using different inflections on various words...employ a pregnant pause somewhere unusual, play with it. Wait a bit, then record it again. Were they the same this time? If they are, then go to longer sentences – then to even longer sentences. These exercises will be invaluable in training your ears. This is known as *'ear training'*, a term commonly used in vocal music training.

Just to give you an idea of what this should sound like, I've recorded a couple versions.

Remember that you'll be reading off a printed page. That page will have **your** markings on it – to remind you to say certain things in a certain way. After your first read, mark it up differently – perhaps print a new page or line so you don't get your markings all mixed up. **PLEASE DO THIS. IT'S A CHANGE OF HABIT THAT YOU MUST EMBRACE.**

At this point, you're approaching the level of not only remembering what you sounded like, but imitating those sounds as you record them again. You're hearing, very precisely, what you said, as you said it! Whatever you say must be passed through a filter. That filter just happens to have ears. Yours. Hope that all made sense. If not, read this paragraph again...out loud perhaps...WOW, what a concept!

Trained singers must incorporate this skill all the time. If they don't they would invariably sing flat, sharp, too slow, too fast, too loud, too soft, etc. Again we don't have to learn anything more about music than the fact that there is a close correlation between vocal production in singing and speaking.

It might sound like trained speakers really have it easy. At least that's what some speakers believe...and that's one of the primary reasons many speakers don't exhibit characteristics of a **trained** speaker. They think, that because they've been talking their entire lives, that's enough. Ain't so.

After you've done this recording thing lots and lots (and that will vary depending on how comfortable you feel with your progress), discard the cell phone, and read passages while intently listening to every sound you're making the very instant that you produce that sound. Oh, it will throw you off your reading skills a bit, but again, do it over and over and over. It's absolutely amazing how you'll be able to alter your vocal production *IN THE MOMENT*, depending upon the current setting/environment/audience.

> ...when you begin to sound boring to yourself, you know your audience is experiencing the same thing.

OK – yes, this might be the boring part. But wouldn't you prefer to bore yourself for a short time, rather than bore your audience for an eternity? And, it can actually be fun – recording, hamming it up, listening, doing it again. You might even get to laugh at yourself. That's a good thing.

**NOTE:** Not all of us are particularly good at telling jokes. However, this is one area that can fast-track your progress as a speaker. Find a couple of good, longer jokes. It makes no difference what the subject matter – just so it's funny, initially to you. You've got to laugh before you can make anyone else laugh. Practice telling the joke. You have a built-in audience. You. Rehearse it. Record it. Tell it to your sofa, your pet, your friend. Use as many of the techniques you've learned in this book as you possibly can. This is where you can exaggerate as much as you like. Make it fun. That's all. Fun! This will have the valuable effect of loosening you up a bit. And that's another good thing.

This ability to listen to yourself, simultaneously while speaking, is really the key to being able to speak effectively, over an extended period of time, without putting your audience to sleep. Think of it in terms of knowing precisely when you begin to sound boring to yourself  you know your audience is experiencing the same thing. You actually become your own audience! You master this and you will become a magnetic, interesting and impactful communicator. Start now. Practice. It's not going to happen overnight...but positive changes *will* occur.

NOTES:

# Chapter 10

## Getting and Keeping Attention and Other Suggestions

How to begin? I don't think there have been more books and articles written about any other subject relating to public speaking. I probably shouldn't waste time on this subject, since there are so many sources out there that will give you all the information you need. However, in keeping with the pretext of what this book is all about – namely how your voice can be used to connect, influence and entertain people – I feel compelled to make some comments.

How do you begin?

Here are some ways that have been suggested – all of which I've used at least once during the past several decades.

1. Tell a joke
2. Tell a personal story – or anecdote
3. Start with a video
4. Show an amazing photo
5. Use a prop
6. Start with a Power Point outline of your presentation
7. State a shocking statistic relating to your subject
8. Ask a rhetorical question or two
9. Quote a well-known author/personality

And there are undoubtedly many more. Creativity is on your side here.

> You get to be the referee, you get to make the rules, you get to break the rules, and you get to determine who wins!

What **is** rather important when deciding which opening to use, is the make-up of the audience. Again, many books have been written about this subject alone. For the sake of this chapter, let's cut to the bottom line. Are they kids, adults, professionals, single interest, women, men, liberal, conservative, or a Heinz 57 variety? In each case, do your due-diligence and gear your initial comments to your audience. You're the one that needs to adapt to your audience, not the other way around...at least at this point. The tables could soon be reversed.

Once you've opened your mouth and gained their attention, it's your game. You get to be the referee, you get to make the rules, you get to break the rules, and you get to determine who wins! Isn't this a great country!

There is only one word in my opinion that will determine how your initial impact will extend throughout your presentation.

## CONNECTION

Picture this. Stand at the podium, look around the room slowly at your audience (or the few people you're addressing). Do not speak. Make certain you maintain eye contact with EVERYBODY. You will notice some people looking away – fidgeting – checking their texts – whispering to their neighbor – and a host of other disruptions. Don't stare at them, just make certain they, as well as all others in the room are aware that you're not going to begin until you have their complete attention. Have a pleasant look on your face. Perhaps even a slight smile. Don't be intense. Don't worry about how long this takes. You'll more than make up for it during your presentation as the "stage" will have been set. You'll be able to relate so much more clearly and they will be so much more attentive, saving considerably more time than what you took at the beginning.

Now come the first words out of your mouth.

They better be something special.

I can't tell you what those words should be – couldn't possibly do that – I'm not there.

I do remember being enthralled by one presenter. After taking the necessary time to silently "Connect" with the audience, he just said, ***"HI."***

There was so much personality, honesty, authority in that one word, that the whole presentation turned into a masterpiece.

OK – so maybe you're not at that level yet. It takes a little guts and lots of practice to do that. However, the time you take to set up those first words also gives you time for a couple deep breaths, relax, calm the nerves and imagine everybody in their underwear. (I know, you've heard that a million times...old school). I actually did that a couple times, and almost broke out laughing. At least I started the presentation with a smile on my face, and it was apparently infectious – had a great reaction.

One technique that I've gleaned from the music industry is simply to breathe. I know, it's something we all really need to do, but what I'm suggesting is a bit different. Before you utter a word – particularly the first time you open your mouth – is to breathe. You're thinking, "Of course I'm going to breathe...I'm going to take a huge breath...it'll calm my nerves!" OK, go ahead and take a big breath. Not a HUGE breath. A big breath. Then DO NOT HOLD IT! Start releasing that breath – breathe out slowly. And, as you're breathing out, utter those first words. Your whole demeanor will take on a calm – and demanding presence. Try it. Practice it. Then do it. I call it "The common cure for the common cold feet," and it has nothing to do with underwear!

> Start releasing that breath – breathe out slowly. And, as you're breathing out, utter those first words.

Now here's one with which some of you may feel more comfortable than others. Somewhere within your presentation, insert a hint of an accent. Choose a well-known accent – one that won't put you on the *politically incorrect* list. A passage may suggest that you adopt a short, five word phrase in a Southern dialect, or a German accent, or just using a little slang to get your point across. You'll be amazed at how this little trick will perk up an audience. Just don't over-do it!

And here's one of my personal favorites. **DON'T MAKE UNNECESSARY MOVES OR JESTURES!**

This is actually quite difficult and I probably need to write a complete book on the subject, but at least I want to give you a taste. I can't emphasize enough how, with a little observation on your part, you will be constantly critiquing speakers, actors, singers, news commentators and anyone making any kind of a formal presentation.

We're all used to using gestures, head movements and body movements to accompany our words. It seems like we want to fit our words into our own little personalized dance. Unfortunately, these kinds of moves, in front of an audience, are repetitive and boring and don't add to your presentation in the slightest. They detract.

I don't suggest you stand up like a statue, looking like there's a rod up your behind. Be relaxed. Make slow movements as you survey your audience – and continue to do that as you speak. But, before you make any kind of a hand gesture, or head movement or exaggerated body movement, make certain that movement is choreographed with the intended meaning of your words.

Extend your discerning observations to include watching speakers and singers who are moving unnecessarily, possibly keeping time with the cadence of their speech or rhythm of the song. Ever see someone beating out the rhythm of their speech with their hand or foot? Unfortunate. Once in a while you'll come across someone who has very slight movement, where each is carefully planned to coincide with an intended meaning. This is admirable and powerful.

It's also admirable if you have aspirations to move into that elite field of presenters.

Let's take a look at a few words/groups of words that you want to avoid at all times. Ready? These are crutches that have either been with us for a long time – or are experiencing their own little fad/moment in the sun. You know what I'm talking about.

Beginnings like:

- *So* (really popular today – wish I had $1 for every time I heard this in the last month)
- *I mean* (gag)
- *Like (exempt if you happen to be a "Valley Girl")*
- *Well* (that's deep - been around a long time!)
- *You know* (what do I know?)
- *Ahhh* (how's that tonsil? I know, you're just trying to figure out what to say next. Prepare better!)
- *Umm (how did this ever start? Why wasn't it Imm, or Emm, or Omm?)*
- *How's everybody today?* (You really want everybody to answer?)
- *Welcome* (I know...this feels warm and fuzzy to the speaker...and I've heard it done rather well – similar to saying "Hi" that I mentioned earlier. But c'mon, I'm certain you can find a more creative way to say it.)

Realize this. You have less than 30 seconds (some say 15 seconds), to win your audience over. So, whatever you say, ***use your voice***, incorporating as many of the ideas contained in this book that make sense to you. Memorize your opening. Rehearse it. Sleep it. Dream it. It will set you on a path of connection that even some of the best speakers wish they could achieve.

Having said that, you must also ALWAYS be present, in the moment, mindful of your surroundings and audience, LISTEN! Obviously, you have an agenda. But that agenda could be greatly enhanced and more aptly communicated if you were given the opportunity to bounce off of something everyone else in the room was witnessing. If the occasion warrants, be spontaneous, reacting to some immediate issue. This state of mind creates a relaxed demeanor – no hyped-up nerves.

One more thing. I'm certain you've heard this before. "Speak with your eyes." Your eyes become one of the most successful conveyors of what you're saying than you could possibly imagine. This will enhance any **CONNECTION** with your audience beyond your wildest dreams. Your eyes must be actively engaged in every word you're uttering. Every word. Yes, this is getting into something more than just the verbal delivery, but goes hand-in-hand, like love and marriage...or a horse and carriage. You can't have one...(you fill in the rest.).

> Your eyes must be actively engaged in every word.

One caveat – sort of. You may be thinking that the image of your eyes reflecting what you're saying won't work if you're in a large room where your audience can't focus on you well enough to see your eyes. If there's a monitor set up, showing you on a huge screen in back or on one side of you, the audience will still see you quite clearly. If not, you might not think about involving your eyes. Guess again. Even if your audience can't clearly see your eyes, by involving your eyes your delivery will be greatly enhanced.

Prove it to yourself. Time to look in a mirror. Talk. First say something without involving your eyes. Then say the same thing, but this time engaging your eyes to reflect the meaning you're attempting to convey. This could involve muscles around your nose, cheeks, forehead and mouth. If this is the first time you've been aware of how important your eyes are in communication, it will feel a bit strange and you'll be amazed at how different you sound. Record yourself. (You should know how to do that quite effectively by now.)

You've made it this far in your reading. You understand quite well that *More than Your Words* is one book among many that has something to do with communication and public speaking. You've also noticed that it's different than any other book available, and addresses different issues. While what is discussed in this book provides the fundamental building blocks upon which superb communication skills are built, the public speaker does require a bit more in order to effectively do his/her thing.

I've previously discussed a couple of areas about which I feel strongly and about how they can be used to your greatest benefit from the beginning. But again, there are countless books covering subjects like how to begin a speech, from entirely different perspectives.

Here are some recommendations regarding publications I feel address various aspects of oral/verbal communication, mostly involving the public speaking arena. Some of these are older books that can be found in your local library. Many of the techniques haven't really changed in years.

If you happen to be a member of **Toastmasters** or any other public speaking support group, they all have their favorite books covering areas not addressed in *More than Your Words.* They're all quite valuable. Here are a few additional publications of which I'm aware.

- "Standing Ovation" by James C. Humes – 1988 – Harper & Row, Publishers
  - o An older book with a more traditional approach to public speaking – covering many of the accepted techniques of organizing your speech, making use of parables and pictures, the art of quoting, how to use visual aids as a prop, not a crutch. Even though this book has lots of miles on it, there are basic truths that will live on. Please do give this book some attention. This book, as well as the others listed, very likely can be found in many libraries.
- "Taking Center Stage" by Deb Gottesman and Buzz Mauro – 2001 – The Berkley Publishing Group
  - o This book could speak loudly to those who have some background in acting. There is a strong correlation between polished public speaking and being a thespian, just as there are many similar techniques that singing has in common with speaking. Even though I've integrated many of the pertinent techniques in **"More Than Your Words"**, if you want a full dose of well-presented material, this would be a good read.

- "Present Like a Pro" by Cyndi Maxey, CSP, and Kevin E. O'Connor, CSP – 2006 – St. Martin's Press, Publishers
  - Since this publication is only 10 years old, I guess it qualifies as being current. It has some rather practical and interesting takes on how to prepare for a speech, as well as the delivery. The chapter that most resonated with me was entitled 'Break the Rules'. That appeals to me a lot. (My wife agrees…)
- "Smart Talk" by Lisa B Marshall – 2013 – St. Martin's Press, Publishers
  - Dealing more with interpersonal relationships at virtually any age level, this book is quite insightful regarding difficult conversations and choosing the right words for the right occasion. With strategies and practical actions plans, *Smart Talk* will help resolve conflicts, strengthen your natural charisma, and assist with the art of persuasion. It's all practical and rather fresh.
- Nightingale-Conant has a plethora of materials available on the topic of public speaking – as well as many other self-help areas. Most of the books and audio presentations have been thoroughly vetted and are quite extensive. Many of the offerings contain multiple CDs and tend to be rather expensive. In order to justify purchasing something of this caliber, you must totally dedicate yourself to a full immersion of information – over a relatively long period of time – and try not to be overwhelmed.

NOTES:

# Chapter 11

## **What happens now?**

One question that I've been asked since writing this book is "How were you able to identify these techniques/methods/procedures that you reference in this book?"

It was a combination of having decades of professional experience in theatre as an actor and director, vocal music, entertainer, choral conductor, voice-over artist, sales trainer and public speaker...and then **connecting the dots**. In my case, connecting those dots meant doing a lot of listening, analyzing, asking questions, being at the right spot at right time and observing various genres of verbal delivery – over a very, very long period of time. In many cases, the realization of what I had observed didn't hit me until well after the fact, and that proved to be quite impactful. I've consolidated these into as concise a format as possible so that virtually everybody can easily and quickly read my thoughts...and...that's the easy part. Assimilating and putting what you've learned into practice is up to you. It takes time and **practice** to put it **into practice**.

If you have the desire, I know you can do it.

Without being judgmental, it's imperative that you continually observe...tune in to how people are talking...everywhere. Whether it's listening in on a conversation at a restaurant (you really do that?...), trying to absorb a sermon at church, attending a seminar on something of interest, participating in a sales training session, watching a TV news broadcast or listening to a radio talk show, think about one of the tenets discussed in this book. You only need to think about one at a time, and apply it to that person's delivery. Then, as you get better and better at analyzing, think about more than one. It's called layering. Remember, it's not about being **judgmental** – but it's important to be very **observing** and **discerning** in order to learn a new way of being. Of speaking. Then applying it to your own circumstance. Your voice will handle it. You just have to convince your mind.

Again, I'd like to remind you to try to disregard the quality of the person's voice. We can't all sound like James Earl Jones, or Barbara Walters. Their DNA was mostly responsible for their sounds, and our ears easily pick up those rich, vibrant tones. Enjoy them. They represent an extremely talented group of people who have chosen to invest their energies on a path that brings them large financial rewards and enjoyment to the masses.

And, please don't try to imitate anybody else's delivery. Just put the rules and techniques you learned here to good use, with your own voice and creativity.

Most of the TV personalities, both local and national, have voices that are not unlike yours or mine. They have, however, developed a certain speech pattern and methodology that apparently works for their station management. I challenge you to spend a few minutes, analyzing the way a local reporter or news anchor delivers his/her message. Remember, usually they're **reading** off notes or a teleprompter, and many of them truly believe that the way to get a point across is to sensationalize virtually every word that has a little bite to it. Have they ever heard about phrasing? I believe their presentation becomes trite, boring, irritating and meaningless after the first few words. You decide. You also might want to tune into a PBS station, and compare styles. Do they use the same delivery methods? Are they more in line with some of the methods discussed in this book?

We can't all become really famous in some discipline where people will pack an auditorium to standing-room-only just to hear us expound on the merits of quantum theory, or how making 3 "holes-in-one" in a row really felt. You will be able to command that same attention – enjoy the same interest – by concentrating on the creative use of your own voice.

If, however, you've reached a level of notoriety where you can go anywhere, say anything any way you want, on your selected subject – or possibly any subject you choose,  if you've persevered and reached this point in your reading, and you're a celebrity of some kind, let me know who you are – and what, if anything, you've been able to take away from this book.

However, you're the only one who can determine what your own path will be when it comes to verbal communication. If you choose to make some changes, it will be imperative that you combine a determined regimen of "Practice" with your "Desire." In some cases, you'll be incorporating rather major changes in the way you've always read out loud and/or talked.

Once you give it a chance, I believe you'll be hooked on making speech pattern changes that will bring you closer and closer to becoming ***one of the Most Interesting Human Beings in the Universe.***

# Dedication

To:

- Those who have inspired me to write this book and those who may benefit from reading it.
- Those who feel ignored when they speak but are willing to find their unique voice and learn how to use it effectively.
- Those who are not afraid to explore ideas that will easily set them apart from their peers, accessing secrets employed by expert speakers, actors, voice-over artists and the rare, outstanding TV news personality.
- My daughter, Meghan Dryw, who never ceases to amaze as she explores her many roles in life: mother, wife, administrator and a never-ending array of theatrical pursuits.

# Acknowledgements

Some of these individuals are no longer with us, but their influence will last as long as there are individuals interested in reading thoughts and ideas passed on by these incredible teachers. I merely serve as their mouthpiece.

**Rev. T. Perry Jones**: the very first clergy I knew in elementary school. He was from England, had a delightful accent, sense of humor, and exceptional delivery. I hung on every word – even when he was reading scripture. I had no idea why. I thought everyone spoke like that. I later discovered he was the exception, and it wasn't because of the accent. **Ralph Percy:** my sophomore English teacher who coached me when I was selected to read a narrative for a high school assembly. The 45 minutes we spent reviewing the scrip is something I remember to this day. The primary idea imprinted on my brain was that each and every word is important, to a greater or lesser degree, and they must all be spoken and smoothly connected in a manner to make an impact on the audience. **Buzz Buscechi:** my college drama coach, teaching me the rudiments of "Method Acting" and providing a full understanding of the Shakespearian quote, *"All the world's a stage, and all the men and women merely players."* **Dave Bryant:** stage director par excellence, with whom I had the privilege of working as both actor and tech director during high school, college and beyond for Summer Stock productions in Wisconsin. He showed me how heart and excellence work hand in hand in creating the ultimate theatrical experience. **Morris D. Hayes:** University of Wisconsin music professor and mentor. He inspired and helped me make the inevitable connection between impactful singing and meaningful speaking. According to

Robert Shaw, he was the greatest men's choral director in the world...and a dear friend of mine in his later years. **John Wilson:** stage director with whom I had the pleasure of serving as music director for numerous community shows – some in an outdoor amphitheater setting where we played to 4,000 people a night. He made theatre more fun than I could have ever imagined. **Clark Eide**: my best friend for over 40 years – knows everything about me – always has an encouraging word – articulate and well-read – a current author – and helps me keep a proper perspective on life. Also responsible for the incredible 5 years of singing and touring with The Fabulous Fourmel'dyhides. (Web page still going strong at www.fabulousfourmeldyhides.com.) **Rev. Patti Paris:** my spiritual leader, wise, always willing to offer practical guidance in times of challenge, has a genuine, down to earth sense of humor, doesn't take crap from anyone, and just happens to be an excellent speaker. **Peter Bolland:** a college professor, musician and spiritual teacher who inherently embodies every element of what interesting speech is all about. **Tim Kasnoff:** entrepreneur, idea person and loyal friend who inspires everyone with his persistence and dedication to helping others. **Lynn Martens:** my loving wife for over 32 years, who puts up with endless hours of looking at my bald spot as I sit at the computer. She also serves as occasional editor...letting me know when I've crossed the line. (What line? There is no stinking line!). **Chris, Hannah, and Nakita**, my 3 Musketeers of editing and publishing at *Publish or Perish.* Thank you!

## Author's Profile

Carl Martens, known in some circles by his stage name, "Doc Martens", has accumulated a lifetime of knowledge and experience relative to communication techniques. His early interest in music, speech and theatre led him to pursue advanced training in piano, voice and stage at the University of Wisconsin. Following his formal education, while continuing as an avocation in the artistic world, he pursued a lengthy career in marketing and sales training for national companies in several disparate industries. During this time he developed a conviction that there is an undeniable correlation between being a business success and an individual's level of expertise in being a strong communicator. How that common thread affects communication through the many techniques embodied in various aspects of the performing arts is his focus in *More Than Your Words*. Besides his primary career path, Carl has continually honed his skill as a performer, professional musician, voiceover artist and public speaker.  Currently, he spends the majority of his time conducting workshops regarding presentation techniques and public speaking in the corporate world. *More Than Your Words* was written after having been repeatedly asked if he had a book (rather than volumes of hand-outs), that could be accessed in conjunction with the workshop.

# ADDENDUM:  Concerns and Responses

1.  **Real Estate Agent** - **Even though I realize this book is designed for people who are involved at some level with public speaking, will it have an impact on those of us who don't have aspirations in this area?  Who is your primary market?**

    The basic tenets of communication as outlined in this book are exactly the same, whether addressing a group of 500, or having a one-on-one conversation with your friend, spouse or children.  If you fall into any of these categories, this book should not only be of interest to you, but will contribute to your speaking effectiveness, on many levels.

    - City Council/Public Works/Planning Commission presenters
    - Clergy
    - Corporate Trainer – in any area
    - High School and College students who strive for success – in any area
    - Lay Reader – Church – other organizations
    - Legal Profession – especially the courtroom lawyer
    - Member of any of a number of organizations that promote public speaking, like Toastmasters, The National Speakers Association, etc.

- Parent
- Politician
- Public Speaker
- Research Scientists/Doctors/all Professionals presenting scholarly papers
- Sales & Marketing Trainer
- Sales Representative
- Seminar/workshop leaders
- Spouse
- Story Teller
- Teacher – at all levels **(One of the most important areas!)**
- Telemarketers

2. **Entrepreneur** - **So, let's not beat around the bush. What's the basic premise of this book?**

   Read the Preface. (Sorry, annoying, I said I'd try to avoid that. However, having said that, I'd prefer if you'd avoid using the word "so" to begin this question – or any other question or statement. One of my pet peeves. Thank you!)

3. **Public Relations Officer** - **Is there a different approach that you would suggest for different professions, or is this a "One size fits all," offering?**

   The material in this book can be easily read, digested and implemented no matter what profession is in question. The basic elements are the same for all. It has nothing to do with what life's work you've chosen.

4. **Attorney** - I consider myself a pretty good speaker – but realize there is always something new to learn. I have a sense that my ego might be bruised a bit while reading and implementing the teachings in this book. Should I be concerned about that?

   I firmly believe that anyone who has the inclination to get up in front of people and make a presentation – of any type – must have a little ego. I promise, no bruising. The important thing is to realize the limitations of your ego, and keep it in tow so it doesn't influence your growth as a communicator or human being.

5. **K – 12 Teacher** - I'm a teacher. Kids all day long. I'm talking all day long. I get very tired of listening to myself, hour after hour. Will what you offer in this book give me a new perspective on my issues?

   More than you can imagine. Not only will your students respond to you in a more positive manner, but you'll actually find pleasure in the changes you'll be making in how you sound to yourself. You will like what you hear…and it won't be monotonous or boring…hour after hour.

6. **Musician & Vocal Coach** - I'm a professional musician (vocalist), and music teacher. As long as I'm teaching one-on-one or performing, I have no problem with focus or nerves. However, periodically, I'm asked to make verbal presentations to groups of more than one. I

**don't like it – and I don't make what I believe is an articulate and interesting presentation. Will what this book presents help me?**

Being a student of music, you already have so many of the techniques discussed in this book locked inside your brain and they're at your fingertips. You're just not incorporating them when you transition from singing to speaking. Once you learn about these techniques, you'll be amazed at how easy it can be to be as impactful a speaker as you are a singer.

7. **Corporate Executive - So many books I've read and courses I've attended on public speaking seem to focus on the same things, organization of material, projection, eye contact, visuals, attitude, movement, dress, gestures, understanding your audience, and a host of other physical and mental aspects of speech making. Is this book going to be a re-hash of all of that again?**

Nope. All that stuff is really, really important, but what we're dealing with here is something quite different. It's the part of the puzzle that needs to be put in place before all those other things can reach their full potential. It's the root of the entire talking/speaking/reading experience. The approach of most books and trainings on public speaking begin with the cosmetic elements rather than the intrinsic details that must first be absorbed and implemented. As you know, in the first chapter, I made a rather interesting analogy to a super model.  Please keep that in mind as you continue to read.

8.  **Sales Representative** - How long will it take to learn what is being presented in this book?

I have no idea.  It depends on your desire, your ability to absorb the book's contents and the time you put in on practicing the various suggested exercises.  It's a short book, but packed with takeaways.  One of the reasons for the "Workshop" format held for corporations and organizations in conjunction with this book, is to maximize the impact through participant interaction over a 3 to 5 week period.  Should this be of interest to you, you can inquire at www.profitsinpodiumpractices.com.

9.  **College Professor** - Why isn't this being taught in schools – high schools, colleges?

It is, sort of.  Starting in high school, if you were involved in theatre and drama classes, speech activities, debate and various music classes, you acquired a limited taste.  These are areas where you'd actually acquire a basic understanding of many ideas presented in this book.  However, it's most likely these ideas have never been adequately translated into your specific speech patterns and are all locked up in a remote cavity of your brain.  You need a key to open that inner sanctum in order to apply what you learned back then, to your current speech/communication needs. This book is that key.

10. **Clergy – Two questions: First, I've attended a class on public speaking in ministerial school. Will this book enhance that teaching – possibly taking my presentation to another level? And question 2: Is this something I could recommend to my lecternist – and other individuals that take part in the service from the platform?**

Most of the clergy that I've known…and that's quite a few…have all had required speaking courses in ministerial school. However, I haven't discovered one course that approaches speaking the way this book does. Not only will you attain a higher level of communicative effectiveness in your sermons, but others who read this book and take part in the service will actually look forward to addressing the congregation, and will do it in such a way so as not to become a weak link from the pulpit. Besides not having convenient parking on Sunday morning, ineffective speakers is one of the main complaints of parishioners today. Time go grow that congregation!

11. **Technical Trainer - Is there more to learning these methods than just reading this book?**

Absolutely. Digest it. Review it regularly. Practice the exercises. Be a constant observer of others' manners of delivery. Find people that desire the same thing and have group chat sessions (and I'm not referring to an online chat room...). Take advantage of a workshop presented where you work or an organization to which you belong. Again, more information about these offerings can be found at www.profitsinpodiumpractices.com.

## 12. **Hypnotherapist** - How will absorbing the ideas presented in this book make me a more interesting person?

Unlike the popular myth that it takes a unique, unusual, large, deep, flamboyant voice or someone with a foreign accent to really be interesting, some of the most "interesting" voices are those that merely incorporate the various approaches contained in this book. So don't get all bent out of shape because you never thought your voice was very impactful or interesting. It makes no difference as to age, gender or quality of your voice. You **WILL** become a more interesting speaker/reader/talker, and people will respond accordingly.

## 13. **Engineer** - I frequently have to outline rather boring details about community development projects – presenting all the facts concerning zoning, EIS, etc., and it seems like it goes on forever. Is there any way that I can keep from putting my audience to sleep?

Absolutely. Even though the material you've been given is admittedly rather "dry," many of the same techniques that apply to presenters who may have more interesting subject matter, will apply to you as well.

## 14. **Advertising Account Executive** - I really don't like the way my voice sounds. How can I get over that?

Hardly anyone likes the way they sound...at first. I remember the first time I heard my voice on a recording. Awful! Just know this. The way you sound to yourself (at least when you first begin listening to yourself), has nothing to do with the way others hear you. The other question that usually follows is, "Can I change the way my voice sounds?" Yes, if you're willing to spend many years and thousands of dollars on voice lessons (or having some 'cosmetic surgery' done on your vocal cords...ouch). So the alternative is to use what God gave you to the best of your ability – along with some proven methods to maximize the effect your voice has on others.

## 15. **Seminar Leader** - I've been told that I need to get more inflection in my speaking. What exactly does that mean?

Incredible question! Inflection refers to the varying of pitch which you invoke as you talk, deliver a speech or read out loud. However, the many books that have been written about public speaking and mention that term, rarely go beyond the statement, "Just work on your inflection." That's like saying to a golfer, "Just go work on your swing." You need to either read a bunch and practice - or have a coach watch you and give necessary suggestions. The same is true in effectively incorporating proper vocal inflection. This book spends considerable time on that issue.

16. **Physician** - I get so tired listening to TV news commentators. What is it about most of them that is so irritating? I thought they're supposed to be professional speakers.

> Now you've opened up a can of worms, and I run the risk of alienating a bunch of TV personalities. However, the response to your query goes well beyond what a short answer will provide. This is actually what this entire book is about...changing the bad habits that make verbalizing very uninteresting.

17. **Law Enforcement** - I'm afraid that if I change my speech patterns/method/whatever it is that you present in this book, that I'll sound affected – fake – not real. Will I?

> If you read this book, and HONESTLY want to follow the techniques suggested, I can guarantee you that you will not sound like any of those dreadful things. Remember, you're not changing your voice at all...just the way you're accustomed to using it. The **WAY** you change how you're using it, as long as you're doing it honestly, will have a very subtle effect on individuals and groups that you address. They won't know why, but **YOU** will be the direct beneficiary of their increased reaction and retention of information.

18. **Public Speaker** – There are obviously many other books written about public speaking. What makes this one different?

You're right, there are virtually unlimited books, blogs and periodicals addressing the various aspects of speech making. Many of them are excellent, and within this book I'll refer to a few that you may want to access. However, they all focus on aspects of how to prepare and organize your thoughts in order to make a meaningful presentation, how to present yourself physically to maximize your presence, how to understand your vocal mechanism, exercises to strengthen your voice, how to analyze your audience, how to make certain the PA system is what you need, etc., etc., etc. To my knowledge, after an exhaustive investigation, this book is the only one of its kind addressing vocal techniques, tying them directly to oral reading, which all the others seem to ignore. It is also the only book that is applicable to virtually everyone on this planet – whether you're involved in public speaking or just engaging a friend in conversation.

19. **High School Student** - I'm a student about to enter college. I've been involved in a little theatre and music – and plan on pursuing a career in communications. Are there benefits that I could derive from reading this book beyond what I've learned from these activities?

You have a good start. Your ear has been trained a bit regarding different styles of vocal production – and you've had an occasional reason to vocalize in something other than your normal, every-day speaking voice. You are probably a bit more receptive than some to listening for sounds that you as well as other people make. You also have the beginning of the ability to discern between various vocal techniques. This book may be a little easier for you than some to assimilate, and will give you the base you need to pursue virtually any type of communications degree...I hope with HONORS!

## 20. College Student - Well-intentioned lectures, motivational speeches and self-help books are usually packed with lots of valuable information. I'm usually so inundated with ideas after the experience, that I rarely put anything to use – and the entire time I spent is virtually wasted. Can you please address my issue?

You've perfectly identified one of my all-time frustrations with any type of self-help content – whether in written or verbal form. There are some individuals who I refer to as self-help junkies – just can't get enough input...but it rarely results in inspired output. All that information is just clogging up the brain's filtration system. When I attend a lecture, workshop or read a self-help book, before I begin to absorb anything, I make a deal with myself to take away at least one idea that I will implement immediately. There are few times when that number expands to five or six...but that's stretching it a bit. I challenge you to do the same here. I have a strong sense that you will identify and implement a limited number of tenets presented in this book that will make digesting this book extremely valuable to your oral presentation. If you only take away and implement one idea, it will provide a solid platform for further study, and your verbal delivery will improve dramatically. Also, since you have the audio files at your disposal, they can be accessed at any time to reinforce any of the techniques with which you wish to reconnect.

Made in the USA
San Bernardino,
CA